160 Top Tips for Public Speakers

By Paul Sloane

Copyright Paul Sloane 2024

Contents

Introduction 5

Preparing your Talk 8

Before you go on stage 31

Delivering your Talk 41

Speaking Remotely on Zoom or Teams 64

After-Dinner Speaking 71

Marketing and Selling your Services 76

Cruise Ship Speaking 94

The Worst Mistakes Made by Speakers .. 101

About the Author 109

Introduction

This book is designed to help a good speaker become a great speaker. It will benefit anyone who wants to speak like a professional. The professional speaker aims to entertain, inform and motivate an audience often with the purpose of galvanising people into action. Speaking involves an element of theatre. It is a performance art which lends itself to an entertainer with a flair for dramatic communication. But it is also a discipline which requires keen preparation and attention to detail. Great speeches which appear natural and spontaneous are usually the result of many hours of preparation and rehearsal.

Professional speakers are constantly in demand for corporate events and conferences. Someone who can challenge, stimulate and energise an audience with strong relevant messages will be offered plenty of well-remunerated work. The tips in this book include many secrets used by successful professional speakers. If you apply them assiduously, they are guaranteed to dramatically improve your speaking performance and your income.

Preparing your Talk

1. Before you start to compose your talk think about the single most important point you want to get across. Audiences cannot absorb a large number of messages. So make sure that your key theme is not lost in a plethora of ancillary topics and stories. Patricia Fripp gives this advice. If you did not have 45 minutes but just one sentence what would you say? That is the central point of your speech. Create your talk around that.

2. Write down various ideas that support your message. Collect different ideas, stories, examples, quotations, facts

and jokes (if appropriate) that relate to and support your theme. You can do this on separate pieces of paper or on your computer. Move them around and consider how to construct your story.

3. Build a structure. Your talk should have a simple and clear structure to it. For example, you might start by stating a problem that affects the listeners. You might explain what causes the problem and why it is serious. You might then introduce your proposal for solving the problem. Then you might finish with a summary and a call to action that lucidly states what you want them to do. Whatever the topic, your talk should build in a

logical way so that your audience can easily follow your train of thought.

4. You should adapt your material for each particular audience but do not write a new speech each time. It is better to have one excellent talk that you love and can deliver faultlessly. Keep your core messages and simply change some examples and stories to make it relevant to the audience. It is easier to find 100 different audiences for one great talk than to construct 100 great talks for the same audience.

5. Add some light and shade. Variety is the spice of speeches. Think about how you can make your talk really

engaging by mixing your approach a little. You do not want dry facts and serious admonitions all the way through. If appropriate add in some humour to lighten the mood. Include some stories if possible – preferably about real people or even yourself. The personal touch can really help to give the talk authenticity and interest.

6. Use your mobile phone to record a video first draft of your talk. It is does not have to be complete and the video does not need to be high quality. Watch the video and you will see many ways in which you can improve your talk. Watch out for mannerisms, hesitations, speed of delivery etc.

7. Watch the video from the perspective of an audience member and ask, 'What is in it for me?' Assess the talk critically to see how much useful value you are providing to the audience.

8. Don't hesitate to use props if they add to your story. This is the spear gun that I used to shoot the shark! Using a prop can break up the talk a little and make it more real.

9. If you get chance carry out a survey among the audience before the event. Sometimes the organiser can send out a short questionnaire. If you are speaking on topic X then ask the

participants, 'What are your three major concerns regarding X?'

10. Some speakers ask the audience about their interests early in the talk. The speaker starts with a strong introduction then stops and throws a question to the audience, 'What are the key challenges you face? What would you like me to address?' This can work well with a responsive audience but can fall flat if you get silence. In this case the speaker continues with their prepared talk.

11. If you are speaking to a large audience then you should stand, move about, use a microphone and be a

little theatrical. If you are speaking to a small audience – say 15 or fewer, then you can be more relaxed and conversational. Sit down and chat with them rather than lecture.

12. If you feel nervous about remembering all the key elements of your talk then use a cheat sheet. Type out the main topics in large font on a single sheet of paper. Have a copy on the lectern and a second copy on a nearby table which contains your props or a glass of water. When you walk over to the table you can glance down at the cheat sheet. Top professionals remember their talk without notes by using a technique

such as the virtual journey which we will cover later.

13. Include humour. Find a style that suits you. Try some funny lines and learn what works. Be careful starting with a joke – it is a high risk strategy but it can pay off. Many speakers shy away from humour because they worry the jokes may fall flat. But it is generally a risk worth taking. Audiences appreciate a speaker who tries to entertain rather than just inform. Choose your humorous lines carefully and then rehearse the words and timing so that you can deliver them with confidence. Self–deprecating jokes are safe bets. Making a joke about some well-known

figure at the conference can work well too but it is wise to check with them first. Of course racist, sexist or offensive material should always be avoided.

14. Humour is good but jokes do not travel well. A funny story that works well in the UK may fall flat in the USA and be considered offensive in Dubai.

15. Include more stories. People relate to stories. If you have an important message to get across about say customer service then you could use charts and graphs and data on customer satisfaction. But it would almost certainly be better to tell a

story about someone who gave great customer service and the impact that it had. Set the scene, describe the characters, tell the story and draw out the lesson.

16. Practise, practise practise. Put your material together in the best way you can and then try it. Practise the talk – preferably out loud. Move things around and drop the less effective points so that the talk really fits together well and communicates the most important points effectively. If possible get someone to listen to your rehearsal and give you some constructive feedback. Check your timing and ensure that you will not over-run.

17. If you do not feel confident about remembering the full talk then use prompt cards. You should not try to memorise the whole talk – just the key headings so that you can remember the main points. The subsidiary material will come to you in a natural way if you know the key topics. If you feel unsure on this then have some prompt cards just in case.

18. If you do not want to use prompt cards, then another good way to remember the structure of your speech is to use the Virtual Journey technique. You take an imaginary journey around a familiar route – say your house and road – and you attach

mental images of the things you want to remember to the places along the way.

19. Analyse your talk for logic and emotion. If it is full of facts and hard arguments then add some emotion – maybe with stories. If it is full of emotion and feelings then add some logic and data.

20. Join a speaker's group such as Toastmasters or the Professional Speaking Association. Go to the meetings to gain feedback on your style and to learn from others. If you want to become a better speak then speak more often. Try out your talk at

Department Meetings, Rotary Clubs, Women's Institutes, Chambers of Commerce etc. The more you practice the better you will get.

21. Try to include the three E's in your talk – evidence, experience and endorsement. If you make a claim then provide evidence from other sources. Mention some of your personal experience to show how you are involved in the topic. Add an endorsement (e.g. a quote) from a recognised leader or expert. These actions all lend credibility to your talk.

22. Include in your talk short quotable statements that are ideal for

retweeting. These are what politicians call sound bites. 'Be remembered, be repeated, be retweeted,' says Patricia Fripp.

23. Make every word of your speech count. Go through your talk and take out every word which is not essential. Include only what is powerful and needed.

24. Watch videos of great speakers so that you can learn from their delivery. (TED is particularly useful.) Watch videos of your competitors so that you can differentiate your approach.

25.   Rehearse and memorise your opening and closing lines so that you can say them faultlessly and with real impact. They are the two most important sentences in your talk.

26.   You need a snappy title for your talk. Bland talk titles do not help you to win business. 'How to improve your Leadership Style' is a dull name for a talk and will not differentiate you from the many other leadership speakers. 'Hire, Fire, Inspire – Get off your seat and start leading!' is better.

27.   Differentiate your talk from those of other speakers in your field. There are many ways to do this

including making your talk more humorous or more personal. Another way is to make it more provocative, challenging and confrontational. You do not want to be just another good, predictable speaker giving good, predictable messages; to be really successful you need a unique angle. Find it. Be different, be unique, be memorable.

28. Investigate the audience. Before your talk find out as much as you can about your audience, their interests and their likely mood. What is it that they will want from your session – information, entertainment, tips, ideas, guidance? What will they have heard or done just before you come

on? Will they be impatient to eat? Will they have had something to drink? The better you understand their needs and attitude the more suitable you can make your speech.

29. If you have to use PowerPoint then minimise these three things – bullet points, text and animations. Use more pictures and the occasional video.

30. If you are using PowerPoint, did you know that you can jump to any part of your presentation by entering the slide number? This gives you flexibility. Say someone asks a question and you want to jump to

topic C which you know is on slide 21 then simply type 21 and press enter. Your presentation will jump there. So, prepare a list of key topics and slide numbers to give you that option.

31. Talk to the Organiser. If you are giving a talk at someone's event then find out what outcomes they want from your session. What are their expectations? What would represent success for them?

32. Investigate the logistics. What is the room layout – theatre style, cabaret style etc.? Will you have a podium, a stage or a microphone? Ask for the things that you might need –

e.g. a microphone, a projector and even a glass of water. Understand the programme and exactly how much time you have. Look at what comes before and after you and make sure that your talk fits in appropriately.

33.   Make it more You and less Me. A big mistake is to make the talk about you, your company, your issues and your achievements. The audience is interested in their problems. You have to make your talk about them. So if you give examples about your company then draw out larger issues and lessons that are relevant and useful to your listeners. Count how many times you say 'I' or 'we' and count how many times you say 'you'.

34. A keynote speech at a conference is often around 45 minutes in length and it should inform, engage and entertain. An after-dinner talk is generally around 25 minutes and should do the same three things but with more emphasis on the entertainment. In planning your after-dinner talk cut down to just two or three main points and include more funny stories and jokes.

35. Spring clean your talk. If you have been giving a similar speech for many years, then you should audit it and replace old material with fresh. Will today's audiences still understand or relate to some of your older

examples and stories? The media coach, Alan Stevens, recommends that you replace up to one-third of your talk every year. Look for new, topical and relevant examples to refresh the talk.

36. Looping is a powerful speaking technique. You start with an idea (expressed in any form) give your talk and then, in your close, you loop back with a link or reference to the original idea. It neatly encapsulates your presentation and looks professional.

37. Prepare for every possible contingency by anticipating worst case scenarios. What would you do if the projector failed in the middle of your

presentation? What if you had an aggressive heckler? What if the microphone failed? Think through every bad possibility in advance and then you will be able to handle any pressurised situation more easily.

38. Prepare a fall-back story or exercise for the audience which you can plug in in case of any calamity – such as forgetting your place or being asked to fill in extra time. If you have in reserve a relevant audience activity then it buys you time to recover your poise.

Before you go on stage

39.　　Always save the phone number of the event organiser into your mobile phone and keep a hard copy before you set off. That way you can let her know when your flight is delayed and the driver who was supposed to meet you at the airport is not there (or any other such problem).

40.　　Give the person who introduces you a concise written introduction script so they position you correctly. The introduction should establish your authority and expertise. It should mention your topic and why you are worth listening to. It should not be long nor full of exaggerated claims about how wonderful and hilarious you are.

41. Always arrive early. Don't catch a plane or train that just gets you there just in time. Catch an earlier one. Arrive at least one hour before you are due to speak. Check the logistics, microphone, stage, video, audio etc. Chat to the organizer to get a good feel for the event and the audience before you set foot on the stage.

42. Before you speak at a conference read their web page to see that you been described accurately.

Study the agenda. Check out the other speakers and link on LinkedIn with any that look helpful to know. They may become future allies or clients.

43.   If you are going to use PowerPoint store your presentation in three places. On your laptop, on your memory stick and in the cloud. (I have had 2 out of 3 not available or working on the day.)

44.   Always have a glass of water near you on stage. Essential if you get a frog in your throat but also useful if you lose your way and cannot remember what comes next. Simply pause and take a sip of water. You will

think of a way to continue and the audience will never know that you forgot your next line.

45. Reinforce your self-esteem by listing all your successes. The longer the list the better so include everything. Read the list when you feel nervous or before going on stage. Every speaker should have their own personal book of successes.

46. Changing your body language can change your attitude and confidence. Before your talk go into a quiet place on your own. Raise your arms high in the air and say something like, 'I will really wow them.'

47.   Use a microphone. For any group of over say 30 and for any after-dinner talk a microphone is vital. It gives you authority, clarity and control. A clip-on is probably best.

48.   Do a microphone check before you go on stage. Please do not start by asking 'Can you hear me at the back?' It is the mark of an amateur.

49.   Check where you can and cannot walk on the stage. You see speakers who wander in and out of the spotlight, stand in the projector image or generate screeching feedback when they walk in front of the speakers. These are elementary mistakes.

50. Dress like a professional speaker. If you are speaking about success and leadership then you should be dressed like a successful leader. This means that you should never be less formally dressed than your audience. If they are in business suits then so should you be. If they are in business casual then you should be in very smart business casual. Find out what the conference leader will be wearing. If the CEO who is going to introduce you will be wearing a suit and tie then so should you even if the audience has many people in open necked shirts.

51. When you are on stage your shoes are clearly visible to the

audience so make sure that they are clean and smart.

52. Check your appearance in a mirror before you go on stage – just in case.

53. Take a spare shirt or blouse with you to every event – just in case you spill something before going on. (And a spare pair of tights if you wear them!)

54. Empty rows of seats when you are giving a speech are a drain on your energy and a distraction. Alan Stevens advises that you arrive early and ask the organiser how many people are

expected. Then count the chairs. If there are obviously too many chairs, request that some are removed. Point out the disadvantages of a half-full room, and the fact that chairs can easily be added at the last minute. If you are able to, it may be possible to switch to a smaller room, or to change the layout from theatre-style to cabaret-style (circular tables with about ten chairs around each). In addition, a few people left standing shows how popular your talk is, which will reflect well on the organiser.

55.   Get your car serviced regularly. You don't want to break down on your way to the gig! Make sure that you

have petrol and water in the car the day before you set off.

56. Prepare all the items you need for the talk the night before you go. Your laptop, memory stick, notes, props, books you are going to give away and so on. Pack your equipment and put out your outfit the night before and you can go to bed unworried. Prepare for success.

57. Just before you go on stage focus on your first couple of lines. Then smile and mount the stage with energy and enthusiasm.

Delivering your Talk

59. It is natural to be nervous. But don't tell yourself you are nervous, tell yourself you are excited. When you first go on stage remember this – nobody wants a bad speaker. The audience is on your side. They want you to succeed. They want you to be brilliant. So fulfil their expectations.

60. Start with a smile. Do not start your talk by saying how pleased you are to be there – that is a cliché. Start with a smile that shows that you are confident and pleased to be there.

61. Your first line should have real impact. Start with a bang. You could offer a startling statement, a provocative question, a remarkable fact, an interesting quote or a funny short joke. Practise this line and deliver it with verve and confidence.

62. If you can make a relevant link to something that has gone before during the conference or to some topical item in the news, then do so. It makes your talk look more spontaneous and up to date.

63. Think of your talk as a conversation rather than as a lecture. Include some rhetorical questions like,

'Do you agree?', 'Has that ever happened to you?' etc. Look at the audience rather than your notes. Adopt a style where you are talking with your audience rather than at them.

64. On stage you should deliberately speak more slowly and more clearly than in normal conversation. There is a natural tendency to rush your delivery. It is especially important to speak slowly if your audience is listening to you in their second language.

65. Don't apologise for losing your place or any such misdemeanour. The audience do not know that you left

out a section of your talk. If you are speaking without notes, then you may well forget some points. But the audience does not know what you intended so put on a brave face and carry on.

66. Be Confident. You will be nervous and that is natural. The best antidote is to rehearse a clear and confident opening to your talk. The audience can read your demeanour instantly. They will be sad to see a quiet, diffident start so please them with a bright, confident opening. Your start sets the tone and a good start will lift you and the audience. You are an expert on your topic so exude confidence in your talk.

67. Look them in the eye. Do not hide behind a lectern or read from your notes. Walk about the stage, look directly at people and talk to them from your heart. Eye contact is important. It engages the audience and raises the level of the talk.

68. Speak Clearly. Your voice is the tool that does the job so use it well. You should not rush or mumble. Use clear short sentences and speak with conviction. Make sure that you can he heard. For larger audiences always use a microphone. Vary your voice. Practise altering the volume, pitch and speed of your delivery. Variety of delivery adds interest especially if it is

done in such a way as to reinforce the message.

69. Use some rhetoric. Barack Obama is a master of using rhetorical devices such as contrast and the list of three. Simple contrasts work well e.g. 'We come not in fear, but in hope.' The list of three items is very powerful e.g. 'We can do this thing, we should do this thing and we must do this thing.' These well-established methods of delivery may sound a little contrived when you practise them but the audience will respond.

70. Pause. The most powerful weapon in the speaker's armoury is the pause. Use it carefully and it will

rivet your listeners. For example, use it before an important item, after a question or before delivering the punch line to your story.

71.   Finish strongly. Signal that you are concluding and then give a simple summary. End with the one clear message that you want people to take away. Give them something to take-away and make it clearly linked to their world.

72.   Another reason to start and finish powerfully is that the event organiser often comes in only for the start and end of your speech. In the

middle she is handling all sorts of last-minute issues. She is the person who will book you again, so it is vital that she sees a strong audience reaction at the start and the finish.

73. Do you really need to use PowerPoint? PowerPoint presentations are the norm but are they the best way to communicate your message? The trouble with them is that they lock you into a straitjacket – you have to follow what is written on the screen. The audience reads the slides and it does not listen to you. Most PowerPoint presentations have too many slides with too much information on each. It becomes a dreary list. Try to condense your

message into a small number of key points and then deliver them directly. Look at and speak to your audience and use very few or no slides at all. If possible replace PowerPoint with directness and enthusiasm.

74. If you have to include visuals then make them dynamic and exciting. Do not overdo the slides – your talk is the primary value and the visuals should be support not distraction.

75. Speak from the heart. Nothing persuades like passion – so be passionate about your message. Personal stories and strong feelings can sway audiences much more than

dry facts and statistics. Of course if you can back up your personal feelings with supporting data then so much the better. But start from the personal – how it relates to you and how it relates to them – the audience. Lessons from personal experience that are relevant to their lives and careers are interesting and powerful ways of holding their attention.

76. The best stories are your own personal stories because only you experienced them and only you can tell them. It is not necessary to start at the beginning. Very often it is better to start in the middle. E.g. 'I was half way up Everest when the blizzard struck.' Begin with an

arresting situation, then you can go back to the build-up. Be sure to finish with the conclusion. The audience wants closure on your story so tell what the result was. And then link it to your theme. What is the lesson that is useful to them?

77. Walk the talk. One of the great things about not using a slide presentation is that you do not have to hide behind a lectern pressing the mouse. You can roam the stage. Walk, then stop, look straight at the audience and ensure eye contact with people. This delivers energy and conviction that can never be achieved from behind a lectern.

78. Vary your pitch. Many speakers deliver their talks in a monotone – same pace, same volume, and same tone throughout. The audience will find it much more interesting if you deploy variety in your style of speech. Your tone should be rich and clear – louder and softer as needed. Sometimes the most powerful points can be delivered in a very quiet voice- with the audience breathless to hear.

79. Keep it Simple. Short sentences and a clear structure work well. Tell them what they are going to hear and why it is important. E.g. 'I am going to give you four key messages that will enable you to double your market share this year.' Then tell them. Finally summarise and reprise the main

points. Finish with a strong and motivational summary. Long, complex presentations may appear sophisticated but often they will lose the audience and little is retained. The best presentations engage the audience with clear messages that are inspirational, powerful and easily remembered.

80. Watch your audience. Are they fully engaged? Are you losing their interest at some point? Which lines make them laugh? Make a note so that you can adjust your talk to improve it for the future.

81. Engage your audience with interactive content. People suffer

fatigue during business conferences. If you have a long talk then ask some questions or include some relevant interactive exercises. Don't ask your audience to do something uncomfortable for the sake of interaction. You will antagonise some people. Any interactive exercises should be relevant, easy and non-threatening.

82. Stay for the whole conference – not just your speech. You will learn from other speakers and gain valuable networking opportunities.

83. If you use a teaser, keep your promise. In the pre-conference

promotion and at the beginning of your talk you can use a teaser e.g. 'in this talk I will share with you the single greatest secret of all successful chefs.' Of course, you have to deliver something worthwhile when you fulfil the promise.

84. Keep to time. Event organizers and audiences do not appreciate a speaker who overruns his allotted time. Worse still, the speaker compounds the error by rushing towards the end to cram in all his remaining slides. If you have a 45 minute slot then practice a talk that fits comfortably into 40 minutes. That way you can end the talk in a strong, confident manner and take the time

to really deliver your key message. If you have time over you can always offer to take questions.

85. When you get a question from a member of the audience, repeat it. There are two reasons. Many members of the audience will not have heard the question and they want to know what you are answering. Secondly it gives you just a little more time to consider your answer.

86. If you do a Q&A session after your talk, do not conclude with the answer to the last question. You want to leave the audience on a high and remembering your key point. Answer

the question and then add a coda. Say something like, 'Just to summarise….' and then give them a brief and dynamic finish.

87. Speak to sponsors and partners. When you speak at a conference try to contact not just the organiser but also the sponsors and partners. Ask which other conferences they support. They might provide additional speaking opportunities.

88. Be available for follow-up questions and discussions. Hang around after your talk to answer any additional questions – maybe from people who did not get chance to ask them earlier. Sometimes these

people prove to be future clients. Have a supply of business cards to give out.

89. If you want some safe interaction, think of some relevant questions for which you know the answers. 'Would you agree that teamwork is important in your business?' Get them agreeing with you. Getting people to raise their hands in answer to a question is a good idea because it changes their body language. You can change the attitude of those who have their arms folded in silent defiance by getting them to raise a hand.

90. Alastair Greener gives this piece of advice – Start where your audience is. They have a set of issues and challenges so start by showing empathy with their position then guide them to the place you want them to reach.

91. It is unprofessional to directly promote your books from the platform. However, there are ways around this. If someone in the audience asks a really good question you can reward them with a copy of your book. Choose someone at the back and ask people to pass the book along to them.

92. Another way to promote your book is to give a copy to the person who will introduce you and ask them to mention it and show it in their introduction.

93. Rehearse key sentences to see where to place the stress. Emphasise nouns rather than adjectives e.g. he was an inspiring, courageous, motivational LEADER.

94. When speaking to a foreign audience who are listening to you in their second language you should speak more slowly and more deliberately. Cut out all jargon, subtle humour and clever constructions. Keep the message clear and simple.

95. Be local, be up-to-date, be topical. Include some local examples and location references if possible. Mention something that it is today's news.

96. After you have given your talk always close the loop by speaking to your client. If she is happy with your talk then politely ask her for a written recommendation (not an endorsement) on LinkedIn.

97. If you ask the organiser for feedback on your talk – either on the day or later – they will always say nice things. So a better question is, 'What one thing could I do improve my talk?'

98. It is often a good idea to challenge your audience and to be provocative in terms of questioning some of the conventions of their business or industry. But take care. Never ridicule or insult your audience, the company, its executive leaders or the conference sponsors.

99. Rehearse. I have said if before, but it is so important I will say it again. Rehearse before the event so that you are confident in your material and know that you will not over-run. Rehearse on the day by getting there early and checking all equipment and logistics.

Speaking Remotely on Zoom or Teams

100. Test your set up in advance. Ensure you have a strong internet connection. Turn off unneeded applications, pop-ups and alerts. Turn off other devices which might take up some of your connection bandwidth.

101. Check your audio and video with a test run. In particular, ensure that you have a good microphone which gives high quality sound. Make sure that you are familiar with the system you are using – Zoom, Teams or other webinar software. Rehearse using

share screen so that you can do it without fumbling or delay.

102. Pay attention to lighting. You should be well lit from the front so that your face is clearly visible. A light source behind you, such as a window, will put you in shadow.

103. Look directly into the camera when speaking and not just at the screen of your computer. Adjust your camera so that it is at exactly your eye level. It is easy to put books under a laptop to achieve this.

104. Be aware of the background behind you. People will scan in and make judgements, so it is better to have a plain background or something looking businesslike – such as a bookcase.

105. If you are using slides, then send a copy of your presentation in advance to the organizer. This is a useful backup in case of technical problems.

106. Unless you are in a group discussion it is best to mute everyone except you the presenter. Otherwise, you will get random and distracting noises.

107. Ask people to keep their video on and occasionally ask people to respond to a question by raising their hands. This small piece of engagement keeps them involved.

108. Have someone else assist you by admitting latecomers and monitoring the chat.

109. Keep your talk shorter and sharper. People have a shorter span of attention when watching a computer screen so get to the point quickly.

110. Break up a longer talk into chunks. Involve the audience with the appropriate use of breakout rooms, chat and polls. If you ask people to post in chat, then be sure to read the chat so that you can respond. Ask for brief feedback from the breakout rooms.

111. Speak directly as if to just one person – not to a large audience. So do not say something like, 'I guess some of you have had this problem.' Instead speak as though to one person, 'Have you had this problem?'

112. It is easy to become robotic when speaking to a remote audience.

Try to inject some energy, enthusiasm and emotion into your talk. Humour is still useful though you will not get the same feedback that you get from a live audience – you will get smiles rather than laughs but do not let that put you off!

113. One benefit of speaking to your camera is that you can put a post-it note with the key topics for your talk just under the camera. You can glance at it as you go along. That is what I do!

After-Dinner Speaking

114. After dinner speaking is different from conference speaking in a number of important ways. But similar principles apply. It is vital that you understand the audience and the timings. A boozy rugby club dinner is quite different from Ladies evening at the Church. Your material should reflect the interests and sensitivities of the audience so the more you know about them the better.

115. Place more focus on entertainment. An after-dinner talk can be light-hearted but still carry a serious message. It should contain a good dose of humour. You can usually

make fun of the big cheese there – the golf club captain or rotary club president - but check with them first that it is OK to pull their leg a little.

116. As you chat to people before and during the dinner you can pick up snippets and stories that you can work into your delivery so stay alert during the small talk.

117. Stay sober. Other people may drink a lot and you will be offered drinks, but I think it is best to abstain. You need to be at your sharpest and wittiest when you stand up to speak.

118.   Be prepared to deal with hecklers. Prepare some responses from things you can find on the internet. The first time someone interrupts you, you can carry on but the second time you should immediately respond with a quick answer or put down. It is a skill which great after-dinner speakers develop.

119.   Stay calm. Timings often over-run with the dinner delayed and the previous speaker droning on. Then people need a break and by the time you stand up some are anxious to go home. Relax, smile and engage them with your cracking first line.

120. Keep it short. The organizer may ask you to speak for 40 minutes but the audience generally does not want you to do more than 20 or 25 at the most. The later you start the shorter you should be. No-one wants to listen to a long speech after 10 pm.

Marketing and Selling your Services

121. You need a website for your speaking business. It should contain videos, photos, testimonials and evidence of your expertise and speaking skills. Study the websites of leading speakers in your field to see how they position themselves and then choose an approach which suits you.

122. When you give a talk try to get a video recording of your talk. If the conference organisers are videoing proceedings then be sure to get a copy. You can use edited highlights as part of your marketing and promotion. You can also analyse the

recording to observe your performance, timing body language etc.

123. Construct a show reel with clips of different talks. It should be less than five minutes long. Once you have a great short video it should be embedded on your home page and on your LinkedIn profile. Put it onto YouTube too.

124. If you get an email asking if you are available on a certain date do NOT email back. Instead pick up the phone and call the prospect to discuss their needs. You are now in sales mode.

125. The price you can charge is not determined by the quality of your speech. It is determined by your reputation and brand. This is why an unknown speaker with a great talk gets a fraction of the fee of a TV personality with a mediocre talk. So develop your brand – with books, blogs, articles, videos and of course great speeches.

126. There is price band of what is reasonable to charge for someone of your standing and reputation. Always quote at the top end of this band. There are three reasons. 1. People associate price with quality and think that a cheap speaker cannot be a good speaker. 2. If your price is too high you can always find a pretext to negotiate

a deal. 3. You will not get gigs every day or every week so make some decent money when you can.

127. You are a speaker and you develop your speaking skills. But you are also an expert in a specific field and you should invest time to develop your expertise in that field. Allocate time every week to reading, meeting other experts and listening so that you keep up to date. In particular look out for topical stories and examples that will illustrate the key points in your speech. Many speakers are using case studies and stories from years ago. Use up to date examples and data. You should be more up to date than your audience.

128.   Your marketing should communicate two key messages for potential clients. The benefits to them of your insights as an expert. The benefits to their events if they use you as a speaker.

129.   Position yourself as a thought leader in your field. Show this by sharing your thoughts and insights in your talks, your books and your blogs. You should blog regularly on your topic. Comment on the blogs of other thought leaders.

130.   Ask for referrals. Go back to the clients you worked for and ask them if they know anyone else who could benefit from your expertise and

services. Referrals are often the best source of new speaking engagements.

131. Establish your credibility and authority by writing a book. Draw on the best elements of your speech and your blogs to construct your own angle on your topic. If possible find a publisher first. Get a list of publishers on your topic areas and submit a synopsis, a chapter list, a sample chapter and a description of the target market. A publisher can help you to position and market the book. They can also secure translation rights for foreign markets. If you cannot get a publisher then self-publish. It is most unlikely that you will grow rich from royalties from your book but being an

author helps enormously in building your authority as an expert and in gaining speaking engagements.

132. Use social media and particularly Twitter and LinkedIn to promote your blogs which reinforce your reputation as someone with useful insights into your field of expertise. Follow thought leaders in your field on Twitter. Follow the followers of these people and many will follow you back. By definition they are interested in your topic.

133. Change your title on LinkedIn to Speaker on [your topic].

134. Search on Google and on Linkedin for 'speaker on [your topic]'. Where do you come on the list? Where do you come on a local search? What are the top people on the list doing better than you? Copy some of their key phrases into your profile and website to improve your search rankings.

135. Use Google Adwords to target people searching for speakers in your field. This is particularly useful if you do not come high on the search. You can target geographically – e.g. just your city or country.

136. Don't claim to be the world's best anything unless you have serious

evidence to support it. Prove how good you are with your talk – not with hyperbole in your introduction.

137. Collect names and email addresses on your website. Build an email list. Offer free downloads on your website in return for email addresses.

138. Send out a regular email newsletter but don't call it a newsletter. Tips on [your topic] is better. Make sure that it is short and adds value for your readers. Avoid overt selling of your services. The purpose of your newsletter is to remind people that you exist, that you are expert and that you speak. But

make it interesting or people will simply unsubscribe.

139. Don't just ask for feedback on your talk – people will only say nice things. Ask someone you respect (such as another professional speaker) to tell you two things they liked and two things that could be improved.

140. One of your best sources of future business is past clients. Contact all the people you worked for say one to three years ago. They may need a speaker again.

141. Allocate time every day for marketing. People cannot book you if they do not know who you are and what you do. You should be contacting potential clients in different ways every day of the week.

142. You should do some free talks at the right kinds of events to showcase your talent and, particularly in the early days, to practise your talk. Try to get in front of the right kind of audience but if you cannot do that still offer a free talk to a local school or charity because speaking is what you do.

143. Get some great professional photos. Sometimes your photo is

what gets you booked. It should look professional and dynamic.

144. To find new clients try searching for conferences that will take place near you. Say the nearest big town is Birmingham then search with these key words - annual conference Birmingham. Look for conferences which are due to take place in say 6 to 9 months' time and where your talk would fit. Then contact the conference organiser by phone or email and discuss their requirements.

145. Construct a one-page flyer on you and your main topic. It must be brief and to the point. It has a photo

of you. It summarises you are and why you are an expert. It lists your main talk topics. It contains some short testimonials. Have it available as a pdf document to send out and as a give-away.

146. Target speaker bureaus and send them your show reel, a photo, some customer testimonials and a one-page flyer on you and your talk. They will want to categorise you as a speaker on one particular topic so make it specific and easy for them. They will want to know your fee range and will lose interest it if is too low. They exist to serve their clients and not to serve speakers so do not expect a great response from them. Contact them by email or phone every once in

a while, with new information or testimonials in order to remind them of your talents.

147. If you get a booking through a speaker bureau then all subsequent work with that client must go through the same bureau. Never deal direct with a client who was introduced by a bureau. Never discuss your fee with a client who has booked you through a bureau.

148. Have a card or sheet printed which contains some valuable information from your talk – e.g. data or key points. Make sure it has your webpage and contact details clearly shown. Leave it as giveaway at the

back of the room or have it inserted into delegate packs. That way people can remember you and easily get in touch.

149. When you get a booking to speak at an event in a distant location search your contacts on Linkedin and elsewhere to see who else you know in that city or region. Search second level contacts. Try to get other speaking gigs there or just business meetings with potential clients.

150. Have a business card printed with your title as Speaker. It should briefly list your topics and of course it has your contact details. Use it

whenever you speak, at conferences and at networking events.

151. When you meet someone new at a networking event always follow up with an email within 24 hours. Gently remind them that you are available to speak at their conference.

152. When you connect with someone new on LinkedIn or other social networking sites send them a message asking how you can help. If you remind them what you offer they may ask you to speak at their event.

153. Remember that every speech can become a better speech and every speaker can become a better speaker. Even after you receive fulsome praise from your audiences do not allow yourself to become complacent. Your content, your delivery and your marketing are all work in progress. Continual improvement is the mark of the true professional speaker.

Cruise Ship Speaking

154. Cruises are booming in popularity. Most cruises have guest speakers on board. The first tip concerns the audience. The people who go on cruises are mostly prosperous, educated and retired. They are not particularly interested in self-improvement, motivation or business topics. So your conference keynote talks on leadership, inspiration and empowerment are not appropriate. Nostalgia, crime, celebrity and the entertainment world are examples of popular topics.

155. You will need to prepare at least eight separate talks of around 40

minutes each. They should be entertaining, easy to follow and informative. Do not give the audience difficult challenges or workshop elements – they are here to enjoy themselves. You need to invest time in developing and rehearsing your talks. They should be supported with high quality images and maybe some short video clips. You should be an expert in all your topics because someone in your audience will be! Include some humour if you can – you are there to entertain as well to educate.

156.   Most cruise lines will not automatically accept your claim to be a brilliant speaker. They will want you

to give a short audition before taking you on. You need to choose your most interesting subject and present it clearly and professionally.

157. When you first board the ship be sure to meet the Entertainment Director. He or she is your boss. They will probably introduce you on stage and may sit in on a talk. Their opinion determines whether the cruise line asks you back again. Listen to their input and be flexible in meeting their needs.

158. The title of your talk is crucial. The ship has a daily newsletter which relates all the entertainments and activities of the day. Your talk will get

a headline and sub-title with location and time. Passengers on the cruise have plenty of choice. They can sunbathe, go for a walk, play quoits, play bridge, dance a waltz, watch the football, have a relaxing drink – or they can come to your talk. If the title sounds fascinating they might show up. If it sounds dull they will not.

159. Start with your best talk. Don't build up to a climax in a series of talks. If people miss the first, they will not come later. Start with your most interesting and entertaining material. That way people will talk about you and your attendances may build.

160. You can sell your books on board with prior approval by the cruise line. If people like your talk, then some will want to buy your book.

161. Most cruise lines provide a free cruise for you and your partner. Some pay a small stipend. Some charge you for your partner's flights. You do not get to choose your cabin. You may be put into crew quarters and an inside cabin. By the time you have paid for all your drinks and extras the cruise will have cost you. If you enjoy cruising then it is a really pleasant experience but it does not pay the rent.

162. Check all the logistics, equipment and props on stage before your first talk. Make sure all your videos work. Have three copies of all your presentations – on your laptop, on a memory stick and in the cloud.

The Worst Mistakes Made by Keynote Speakers

163. Here are the worst sins that speakers commit. Be sure not to make these mistakes. First, a weak start. The initial impression that you make on the stage is very important. It should be positive and animated. Many speakers make a feeble start. They look down and mumble their first words or worse still, they make an apology. The audience wants you to succeed. They want you to be professional, informative and entertaining. So meet their expectations.

164. Do not overuse PowerPoint. Slides can be useful – especially for showing charts or images. But many speakers load up their presentation with too many slides containing too many words. Then they read the slides. The audience reads the slide and does not look at the speaker. This is what's known as, 'death by PowerPoint'.

165. There is no clear message. Often speakers try to cover too much ground. They overload the audience with data. There are many different messages but there is no clear theme. Ideally your talk should have one central idea. And your talk should

have a structure that communicates the idea.

166. No Human Interest. Many talks are crammed full of facts, data, charts and statistics. They are dull. There are no stories. People relate to stories about people. So if for example, you want to improve customer service do not drone on about the percentage of net recommenders. Tell a story about someone who gave great service. Describe them and the situation. Make the story come alive.

167. Lack of enthusiasm. A speaker who lacks enthusiasm cannot generate enthusiasm in the audience.

Many speakers deliver their content in a dreary monotone, reading dry statements from a script. They send the audience to sleep. Your job as a speaker is to inform and entertain. You should look the audience in the eye and speak from the heart. Walk about the stage (but not too much). Vary your voice – pitch, speed of delivery and volume. Try to include some humour or something interesting and unusual; but keep it relevant to the topic.

168. Too much of me and not enough of you. A big mistake is to make the talk about you, your company, your issues and your achievements. The audience is interested in their

problems. You have to make your talk about them. So if you give examples about your company then draw out larger issues and lessons that are relevant and useful to your listeners. Count how many times you say 'I' or 'we' and count how many times you say 'you'.

169. No rehearsal. Many speakers make elementary mistakes on stage. They struggle with the equipment. Things they should have checked do not work. Their slides are out of order. It is clear that they have not rehearsed. You should practice your talk before the event so that you can be confident about every aspect of it. On the day of the event you should

check all the equipment on stage and be familiar with all the logistics.

170. Overrunning on time. This is a sin that many speakers commit. Event organizers and audiences do not appreciate a speaker who overruns his allotted time. Worse still, the speaker compounds the error by rushing towards the end to cram in all his remaining slides. If you have a 45 minute slot then practice a talk that fits comfortably into 40 minutes. That way you can end the talk in a strong, confident manner and take the time to really deliver your key message, If you have time over you can always offer to take questions.

171. No conclusion or call to action. The final line of your talk is the most important line in the whole thing. But many speakers fade away with a quiet, 'thank you for your attention'. Finish with a strong, memorable message for the audience to think about and take-away.

About the Author

Paul Sloane gained a first class degree in Engineering from Cambridge University. He was an engineer, salesman and marketing manager at IBM. He went on to become a Marketing Director, Managing Director and CEO of software companies. He is a leading speaker, author and consultant on lateral thinking and innovation. He has written over 20 books which have sold over 2 million copies in total. His top business book is The Leader's Guide to Lateral Thinking Skills. He runs leadership master classes on lateral thinking and innovation with top corporations around the world, including Bayer, Glaxo Smith Kline, Microsoft, Nike, Novartis, Pirelli, PWC, Reckitt Benckiser, Swarovski and Unilever. He has been a visiting lecturer at Cambridge

University, Lancaster University, Henley Business School and the Mumbai Institute of Technology. His Tedx talk entitled 'Are You Open-Minded?' is on Youtube.

Paul plays chess, golf, tennis and pickleball. He and his wife, Ann, live in Sunningdale in England. They have three daughters and seven grandchildren.

www.ingramcontent.com/pod-product-compliance
Lightning Source LLC
Chambersburg PA
CBHW052329220526
45472CB00001B/331